RABINDRANATH TAGORE

RABINDRANATH TAGORE, THE YOUNGEST BUT ONE CHILD OF MAHARSHI DEBENDRANATH TAGORE, WAS BORN ON MAY 7, 1861, AT JORASANKO MANSION IN CALCUTTA.

SHORTLY AFTER RABINDRANATH'S BIRTH, HIS FATHER TRAVELLED A GREAT DEAL AND WAS RARELY AT HOME.

HIS MOTHER, SARADA DEVI, WHO HAD TO MANAGE THE HUGE JOINT FAMILY, NATURALLY FOUND IT HARD TO TAKE PERSONAL CARE OF LITTLE RABINDRANATH.

ISWAR, TAKE RABI AND KEEP HIM AMUSED.

COME, LITTLE ONE.

AND LITTLE RABI WOULD COME DOWN TO EARTH.

AT HOME, THE SCHOOL BECAME HIS MAKE-BELIEVE WORLD WHERE HE WOULD BE THE TEACHER AND THE WOODEN RAILINGS HIS INATTENTIVE STUDENTS.

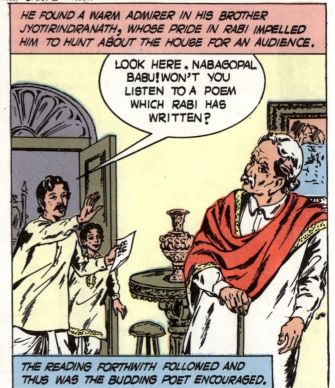

THOUGH RABI DISLIKED SCHOOL AND PLAYED TRUANT, IT DID NOT HARM HIS GENERAL EDUCATION MUCH. FOR HIS HOME WAS A VIRTUAL UNIVERSITY; THE HOUSE OF THE TAGORES BEING A MEETING GROUND FOR POETS, SCHOLARS, MUSICIANS AND MEN OF SCIENCE AND PHILOSOPHY—EACH A UNIVERSITY IN HIMSELF.

WHEN RABI WAS ALMOST TWELVE YEARS OLD, MAHARSHI DEBENDRANATH CAME HOME FROM A LONG SOJOURN IN THE HIMALAYAS.

WHILE I AM HERE, LET THE BOYS BE INVESTED WITH THE SACRED THREAD.

FOR DAYS TOGETHER, RABI AND TWO OTHER BOYS WERE TAUGHT TO CHANT, IN CORRECT ACCENTS, RELEVANT SELECTIONS FROM THE UPANISHADS.

FINALLY, WITH SHAVEN HEADS AND GOLD RINGS IN THEIR EARS, THE THREE WENT INTO A THREE-DAY RETREAT.

THOUGH THE BETTER PART OF THOSE THREE DAYS WAS SPENT AS BOYS WOULD...

...RABI WAS SERIOUS REGARDING MEDITATION AND WAS OFTEN MOVED AT THE END OF IT TO TEARS OF BLISS.

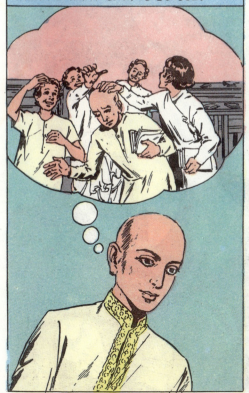
THE EXCITEMENT OF THE THREAD CEREMONY OVER, RABI WAS FACED WITH THE PROBLEMS A SHAVEN HEAD WOULD CREATE WHEN HE WENT BACK TO SCHOOL.

WHILE HE WAS WORRYING OVER THIS, HIS ANXIETY WAS RELIEVED BY AN UNEXPECTED OFFER FROM HIS FATHER.

RABI, WOULD YOU LIKE TO ACCOMPANY ME TO THE HIMALAYAS?

OH! I'D LOVE TO.

FROM SHANTI NIKETAN, THEY WENT TO AMRITSAR AND FROM THERE TO THE HIMALAYAS. IN THE EVENING, RABI WOULD SING SONGS TO HIS FATHER.

AS NIGHT FELL AND THE STARS BLAZED OUT—

THAT IS THE POLE STAR. CAN YOU SEE IT?

YES, FATHER.

RABI'S EYES HAD NO REST THE LIVELONG DAY, SO GREAT WAS HIS FEAR LEST ANYTHING SHOULD ESCAPE HIM.

AFTER HIS RETURN FROM THE HIMALAYAS, HE CONTINUED WITH HIS COMPOSITION OF POETRY. ONE DAY AT CHINSURA, NEAR CALCUTTA, HE SANG SOME OF HIS SONGS TO HIS FATHER.

DEBENDRANATH TAGORE WAS VERY HAPPY.

IF THE KING OF THE COUNTRY HAD KNOWN THE LANGUAGE AND COULD APPRECIATE ITS LITERATURE, HE WOULD DOUBTLESS HAVE REWARDED THE POET. SINCE THAT IS NOT SO, I SUPPOSE I MUST DO IT.

THE REWARD WAS A CHEQUE FOR FIVE HUNDRED RUPEES!

*Bankim Chandra Chatterjee, the famous Bengali writer.

* RETREAT

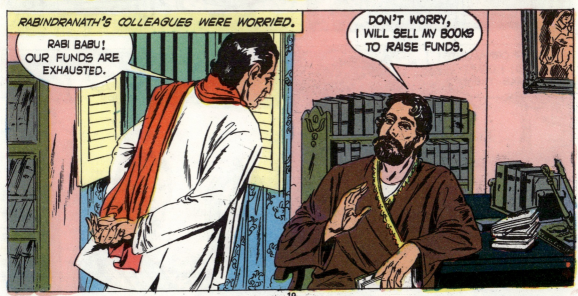

RABINDRANATH TAGORE

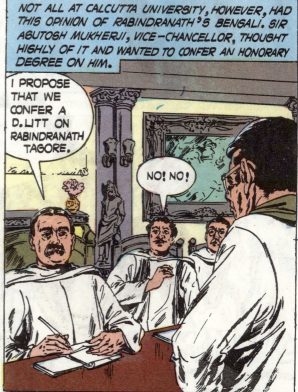

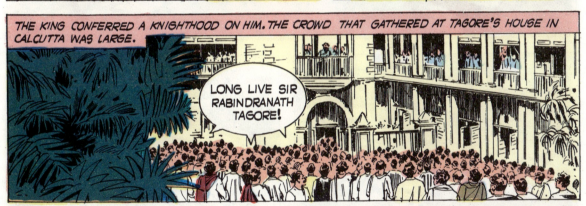

RABINDRANATH WAS DEEPLY INVOLVED IN HIS GREAT EXPERIMENTS IN EDUCATION AT SHANTI NIKETAN. BUT HE COULD NOT KEEP HIMSELF ALOOF FROM POLITICAL HAPPENINGS. THE OPPRESSIVE MEASURES OF THE BRITISH HAD MADE MAHATMA GANDHI GIVE THE CALL FOR HARTAL IN 1919. SEVERAL HUNDRED MEN AND WOMEN HAD GATHERED AT JALLIANWALA BAUG, IN THE PUNJAB. SUDDENLY—

TAGORE WAS SHOCKED AT THIS BRUTAL MASSACRE BY THE BRITISH.

I MUST DO SOMETHING TO ASSERT MY STAND.

HE WROTE A LONG LETTER TO THE VICEROY OF INDIA RELINQUISHING HIS KNIGHTHOOD AS A PROTEST AGAINST THE BARBAROUS ATTACK.

...THE DISPROPORTIONATE SEVERITY OF THE PUNISHMENT INFLICTED UPON THE UNFORTUNATE PEOPLE AND THE METHOD OF CARRYING IT OUT, WE ARE CONVINCED, ARE WITHOUT PARALLEL IN THE HISTORY OF CIVILIZED GOVERNMENTS AND THESE ARE THE REASONS WHICH HAVE PAINFULLY COMPELLED ME TO ASK YOUR EXCELLENCY TO RELIEVE ME OF MY TITLE...

HIS RENUNCIATION OF THE KNIGHTHOOD WAS DECLINED BUT HE STOPPED USING THE TITLE.

THE GOVERNMENT WAS FORCED TO AGREE TO THE MAHATMA'S DEMAND FOR A COMMON ELECTORATE BETWEEN CASTE HINDUS AND HARIJANS. THE MAHATMA BROKE HIS FAST BY SIPPING LIME JUICE, WITH TAGORE SINGING HIS FAVOURITE SONGS FROM THE GITANJALI.

NOW THAT RABINDRANATH HAD ATTAINED WORLD FAME, SHANTI NIKETAN BECAME A CENTRE OF PILGRIMAGE NOT ONLY FOR INDIANS, BUT FOR PEOPLE OF OTHER COUNTRIES AS WELL.

Couldn't find the **Amar Chitra Katha** title you wanted in the store next door?

Log on to www.theackshop.com where ALL the titles are just a click away

90 million copies of over 400 titles sold in the last 40 years